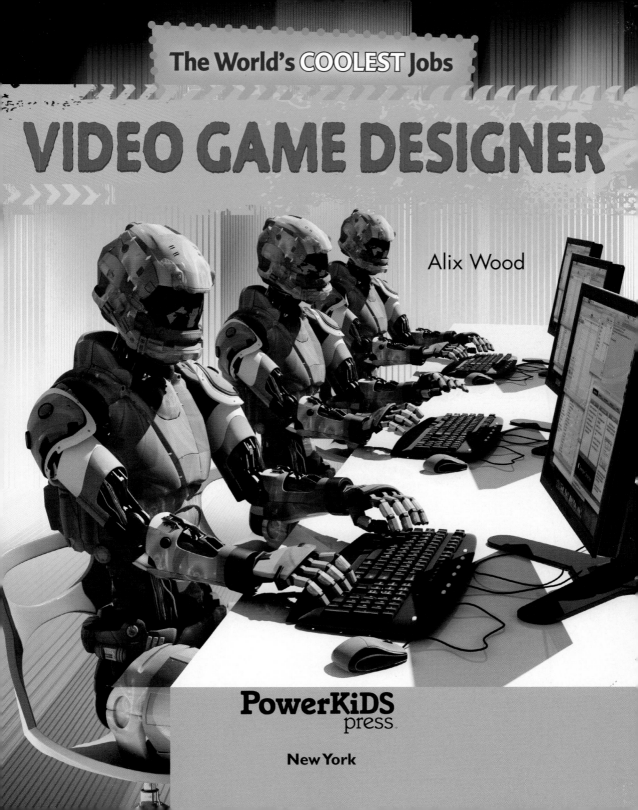

# The World's COOLEST Jobs

# VIDEO GAME DESIGNER

Alix Wood

**PowerKiDS** press

New York

Published in 2014 by The Rosen Publishing Group, Inc.
29 East 21st Street, New York, NY 10010

Editor for Alix Wood Books: Eloise Macgregor
Designer: Alix Wood
US Editor: Joshua Shadowens
Researcher: Kevin Wood

Photo Credits: cover, 1, 5 © Barone Firenze/Shutterstock , 6 top, 8, 9 bottom,
12, 13, 14, 15, 16, 18 © Nick Fury/Shutterstock, 19, 21 © Barone Firenze/
Shutterstock, 22, 24, 25, 26, 27, 28, 29 © Shutterstock; 4, 7 top, 11 inset,
13 inset, 17 right © public domain; 17 left © D. Gordon E. Robertson; 7 bottom,
9 top, 11 © Dreamstime; 6 bottom, 10 © author; 20, 21 inset © Evan-Amos;
23 © Defenseimagery.mil

Library of Congress Cataloging-in-Publication Data

Wood, Alix.
 Video game designer / by Alix Wood.
     pages cm. — (The world's coolest jobs)
 Includes index.
 ISBN 978-1-4777-6015-4 (library) — ISBN 978-1-4777-6016-1 (pbk.) —
ISBN 978-1-4777-6017-8 (6-pack)
1. Video games—Design—Vocational guidance—Juvenile literature. 2. Video games
industry—Vocational guidance—Juvenile literature.  I. Title.
 GV1469.3.W66 2014
 794.8—dc23

                                    2013027475

Manufactured in the United States of America

CPSIA Compliance Information: Batch #W14PK2: For Further Information contact Rosen Publishing, New York, New York at 1-800-237-9932

# Contents

# What Is a Video Game Designer?

People who create new video games are called video game designers. They decide what a game will be about and how it will look. They may design games for computers, game **consoles**, or cell phones.

Video game designers must be creative and have great imaginations. It is their job to imagine brand new worlds and then translate those worlds into games. They need to have good skills in both art and computer **programming**.

## FACT FILE

The first video game to become popular with many people was called *Pong*. It was designed by Allan Alcorn for a company called Atari. Players moved table tennis paddles up and down the screen to hit a ball back and forth with an opponent. The goal was to score the most points. *Pong* may be simple by today's standards. When it was released in 1972, though, it was like nothing anyone had ever seen!

Being a video game designer may sound like a lot of fun. However, it can mean a lot of hard work, too. Video game designers often work long hours and must work even harder when they are close to a **deadline**. Most designers choose this job because they love video games. They do not mind working hard on something they care so much about. It is very rewarding to be involved in creating a game that will be played by thousands of people.

Videogamers waiting in line to play *Call of Duty* at a video games exhibition.

# Pioneers of Play

Today we can play games on cell phones and other devices that fit in our pockets. Sixty years ago, though, that was not the case.

The first computer designed to play a game was called NIMROD. Its display was 5 feet (1.5 m) tall and 12 feet (3.7 m) wide! NIMROD was built in 1951 to play an electronic version of an ancient game called *Nim*. Another early game, built in 1958, was called *Tennis for Two*. It was invented by a physicist named William Higinbothan as a way to interest people in the work that his laboratory was doing.

OXO was the first digital graphical game to run on a computer.

👍 **THAT'S COOL**

One early electronic game used a computer to play tic-tac-toe. *OXO* was designed by A.S. Douglas as part of his Ph.D study at the University of Cambridge, in England. He designed the game to show how humans interacted with computers.

Many of these early games were created to show what a computer could do, and not for the fun of gaming. That changed in the 1970s, though. Games such as *Pong*, *Pac Man*, and *Asteroids* became popular in **arcades**. The first home game consoles were also released in the 1970s. As more people began playing video games, game designers began creating better **graphics** and more interesting story lines. Game designers now needed to have an eye for artistic design and a flair for storytelling, as well as a knowledge of computer programming and math.

# Different Types of Games

In the early days of video games, most people played on machines located in video arcades. Nowadays there are many more types of video games.

Arcade games were built into large cabinets and each cabinet generally played only one game. Arcade gaming is still an important part of the video game industry. It is very popular in Japan and is becoming more popular once again in the United States.

👍 **THAT'S COOL**

There are five main types of gaming.
1) arcade gaming
2) computer and television gaming
3) mobile phone gaming
4) online gaming
5) gaming for training

In the 1980s and 1990s, game consoles got smaller and gaming at home became popular. Computer and television games could be played on consoles and home computers. Today mobile phone games can be downloaded as apps and played on cell phones and mobile devices, such as iPods. They are often free, or just cost a few dollars. They are usually quite simple and designed to be played in short amounts of time.

Video arcades reached their peak of popularity in the 1970s and 1980s. Modern arcade video games may have features such as motorized seats and surround sound to make the experience more fun. Some games are based on television game shows. Players can win tickets for answering questions correctly. They can then cash in those tickets for prizes at the arcade. Arcades often feature many other types of games as well, such as air hockey, skee ball, and claw cranes.

Training games were developed by the US military to teach soldiers about combat situations. They are now used to train many workers, including pilots, forklift operators, and surgeons. There are many educational training games for children.

When playing online gaming, players can work with or compete against players from all over the world.

# Getting Started

With so many different types of games, video game designers need a wide range of skills. They need to be very knowledgeable about computers and computer programming. They also need to understand how different game consoles work.

Video game designers should have very strong math skills and be comfortable with math **concepts**, such as geometry. This helps them draw and design realistic characters, buildings, and vehicles. Game designers also need to know how to translate their drawings and ideas onto computers. Many successful game designers study computer science or computer engineering in college. They learn to work with many different programming languages, such as C++, Java, and Visual Basic.

*Space Invaders*, shown in the background, was one of the first modern video games. Despite its simple graphics, it helped turn video games into a global industry.

A degree is a requirement for many video game designer jobs. Many companies prefer their designers to hold master's degrees. That can mean spending as many as six or seven years of higher education. Some colleges and universities offer programs specifically to train video game designers. Students in these programs study 3D modeling, character design, and **animation**. They also put together a **portfolio** of their best work to show future employers what they can do.

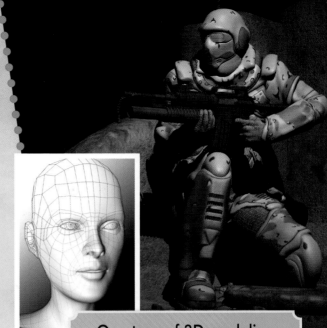

One type of 3D modeling uses a mesh of polygon shapes to form objects, which can then be rendered.

# Creating a Concept

A good game begins with a good concept, or idea. Some games build on concepts that have already proven to be popular in other games. Other games introduce brand new concepts and styles.

Video games come in many different **genres**. There are sports games, strategy games, and role-playing games, for example. Once designers decide what type of game they would like to create, they must come up with a story, or **narrative**, for the game. In a first-person shooter game, the main character may be the last survivor of a nuclear accident, perhaps. The designer will need to figure out what happens to the character during the game and what goal the character is trying to reach during play.

The designer will also need to create other characters for the main character to interact with. Some characters may be **villains** who the hero must defeat. Other characters may give the main character information, such as which direction to go or what weapons to use.

a video game hero

Shooting and action games are not the only types that use narratives. *Rock Band* is a popular music game in which players use controllers modeled after musical instruments and sing. While the fun of the game comes from playing songs, there is still a story within the game. If a player's band performs well, they unlock achievements and play larger and larger shows around the world.

## 👍 THAT'S COOL

Some colleges and universities teach storytelling and narrative design in their video game design programs. Taking storytelling and writing classes can help video game designers learn more about creating characters and plot. It can also help them learn to write dialogue that sounds realistic.

a video game villain

# Finding the Look

One of a video game designer's biggest responsibilities is deciding on the look of a new game. Some games are designed to look very realistic. Others use a cartoon-like style. If a game features fantasy characters, the designer decides what they will look like and how they move.

Sometimes the job of designing and sketching parts of a game will be done by several different people. For example, character artists will draw the game's characters, while a background artist will design the world through which the character moves. The drawings will be submitted to the game's lead designer for approval. The lead designer will make sure that all characters and backgrounds fit into his or her vision of the game.

Video game designers almost always work with several other designers on a project.

Video game designers also plan out what images players will see onscreen. This is done through **storyboarding**. A storyboard is a series of rough sketches of what will appear onscreen when a player moves. If the game's main character encounters a giant monster, a storyboard might show the creature towering above the game's hero. Artists will later go back to the storyboard when they are creating the final images for the game.

## FACT FILE

*Myst* is an adventure game released in 1993. It was the best selling computer game of the 1990s. *Myst* was designed by Robyn and Rand Miller. The brothers spent months designing the look and puzzles of the game. Though it had little action, *Myst* is remembered for its beautiful graphics and design. In fact, in 2012 *Myst* was included, along with a selection of other video games, in an exhibit at the Museum of Modern Art, in New York City.

## 👍 THAT'S COOL

When video games first became popular, televisions and computer screens did not have the technology to make characters and worlds look realistic. Characters were made up of only a few **pixels**, or units of data in a video image. Designers were able to add very few details. Today an image can be made up of thousands of pixels which allows designers to create more lifelike characters.

# Animation on the Move

The first video games were two-dimensional, or 2D. Characters and objects could only go up and down or right and left. Today, many games are three-dimensional, or 3D. The third dimension is depth, allowing characters to move forward and backward in a space.

To create a 3D character, a drawing of the character is scanned into a computer. Designers then use this sketch to build a skeleton of the character. This gives the character its shape and marks points on the body that can be animated, or made to move. Next, a covering, or skin, is put over the skeleton. Finally, artists add color and **texture** to the skin.

The skeleton mesh (left) is then covered with a textured skin (right).

Another animation method is called motion capture. In this method, actors are filmed from all angles while they perform scenes from the game. The actors wear special suits that allow computers to turn their movements into 3D animation.

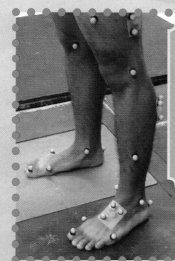

Reflective markers for motion capture can be worn on the skin or on a suit.

## FACT FILE

The 2011 video game *L.A. Noire* used a technology called MotionScan to create its characters. Actors were filmed by 32 cameras, and the video was processed in a computer to create 3D models of the actors' faces and facial expressions. As part of *L.A. Noire*'s gameplay, characters must decide if suspects and witnesses are telling the truth based on their facial expressions.

## 👍 THAT'S COOL

Sports games often use motion capture technology to make players' movements look realistic. The *Madden NFL* video game series films former college and NFL football players running plays that will be featured in the game. The players wear suits that reflect light back to the cameras, allowing the players' movements to be turned into 3D computer images.

# Sounds Great!

An important part of creating a video game is adding the **audio**, or sounds. Audio includes sound effects, voices, and music.

The people in charge of adding audio to video games are called audio designers, audio engineers, or sound designers. Their job is often separate from the job of game designer. However, the game designer will be very involved in making sure the audio sets the right mood and fits the design and concept of the game.

## THAT'S COOL

Most voice actors are unfamiliar to the general public, though their voices may be quite well known. Sometimes companies hire famous actors for voice work.

Actor Samuel L. Jackson did the voice for the character Nick Fury in the video game of *Iron Man 2*.

Most modern games make great use of sound effects. These can be the sounds of closing doors, running water, explosions, or any other sounds that make the world of the game seem more real. Effects may be added by recording a new sound or selecting pre-recorded sounds from a library. Effects such as echoes, muffling of sounds, and noises getting louder and softer are added by the audio designer.

Voiceover actors record their lines in recording studios. Audio engineers then add the recordings to the games.

sound studio

recording equipment

audio designer

## FACT FILE

Video games originally had little or no audio. As technology got better, though, video and computer games had enough space to include music and sound effects. Today, some video games use popular songs, while others have music composed, or written, specifically for them. Sometimes the soundtrack to a video game can be bought separately on cd!

Some video game composers even performed their music pieces with symphony orchestras to sold out crowds!

# Console Technology

Video game designers try to stay ahead of others by developing games using new technology. It is important for designers to be familiar with popular game consoles. Designers should know how the new consoles work and what types of games can be played on them.

Until recently, players pressed buttons or moved joysticks on controllers to send commands to the video game they were playing. That changed with the invention of Nintendo's Wii console. The Wii used controllers and a sensor bar to recognize players' movements.

A Wii remote control (right) and a nunchuk (left). The wrist band stops a player from accidentally throwing the remote control while they play.

In 2010, the Xbox Kinect took this technology one step further. The Kinect did not use controllers at all. Instead it used light, sensors, and cameras to recognize the movements of a player's body. This new technology has opened up new possibilities for game designers. The Kinect also understands voice commands. Microphones in the sensor bar can pick up sounds from several feet (m) away.

Motion sensor technology can make games that involve sports or dancing even more interactive and fun!

# Gaming to Learn

Many video and computer games are designed simply to play for fun. Some games, though, are designed for a higher purpose. Some may teach children math or reading skills, and others may train airplane pilots to fly!

Educational games use graphics, puzzles, and rewards to help people learn new skills. Children as young as two or three years old are able to use simple controllers to play educational games. In fact, many of the top-selling apps on iTunes are made for toddlers and preschoolers. In 2009, a game designer named Katie Salen opened a school where many of the school's lessons are designed like games, with students reaching levels of achievement instead of earning grades.

A toddler playing with a tablet.

In educational gaming, players will often need to master a certain skill before they are able to move on to the next level. They receive instant feedback on their performance and can earn rewards, such as points, for mastering skills. Players must be able to make different decisions and learn from their mistakes. Because of that, game designers will need to create hundreds or thousands of possible game paths. Many designers work with teachers to develop games that teach age-appropriate skills. Designers can even arrange for groups of kids to act as game testers!

A pilot trains in a flight simulator which recreates an aircraft cockpit. The simulator can create almost any scenario that might take place while flying.

# Games Accessible for All

Video games are popular with everyone. Clever adaptations to the controls can allow people with most physical **disabilities** to join in the fun, too.

Video games can create a sense of community by allowing people to play online with others. This can be important to people with a disability, especially if they have to spend a lot of time indoors.

## 👍 THAT'S COOL

*World of Warcraft* is a multiplayer online role-playing game. Many people with disabilities enjoy playing these types of games. Players create avatars and can communicate with each other and often form friendships with other players.

Video games can help children communicate with others even when they normally find communicating to be difficult.

Researchers have found that video games can be very helpful to people with autism. Autism can affect a person's ability to communicate with, and deal with other people. Around one in every fifty children has a form of autism, some more severe than others. There are several mobile apps available that help people with autism to communicate. Some apps have a text-to-speech feature, which allows the device to speak the words that a person types. Others use pictures to help people form sentences and express themselves.

# Making Connections

Video game technology is constantly changing. Designers need to be aware of what is happening in their industry. **Conferences** and conventions are great ways to stay up-to-date and meet other video game designers.

The Game Developers Conference is a large meeting of professional game developers. It was started in 1988 with just 27 designers. Today, it is a five-day event and attracts thousands of designers, artists, computer programmers, audio engineers, and others. The conference features speeches, **tutorials**, lectures, and discussions. Awards are given for the year's best games, too. There is also an Independent Games Festival, open to anyone at the conference.

 👍 THAT'S COOL

The Game Developers Conference has become so popular that it has expanded to other countries. There are now Game Developers Conferences in Germany, Canada, and China!

Sci-fi and fantasy conventions offer video game companies and independent designers a chance to promote their new games. Popular conventions can get over a hundred thousand attendees. They usually stage several different special events, many of them related to gaming. Companies give short demonstrations of their games and allow people to play games that have not yet been released. Conventions also offer designers a chance to talk to players and find out what they are looking for in games. This information can be very useful when they design their next game.

Nintendo fans dressed as game characters march in the annual DragonCon parade, the largest sci-fi convention in the world.

## FACT FILE

In addition to the Game Developers Conference, there are smaller conferences, conventions, and discussions held around the world. Attending conferences is a great way for video game designers to **network,** or stay connected, to other designers and members of the industry. Designers can share any problems that they are having and can learn from each other.

# Still Want To Be a Video Game Designer?

If you have a talent for art and math and a love of video games, becoming a video game designer can be a great choice of career!

The best part about becoming a video game designer is that you do not need to wait until you finish college or get hired by a large company to start. Many designers began creating games when they were kids. Today, technology can make game design even easier. There are many programs out there to let you design your own video and computer games and share them with others.

## 👍 THAT'S COOL

Programs such as GameMaker and Stencyl can be downloaded for free from the Internet. The programs can let you begin designing games even before you master computer programming.

Companies who hire video game designers are looking for someone with good problem solving skills and patience. There are a great many bugs and potential problems when designing a game. *Big Rigs: Over the Road Racing* is regarded as one of the worst video games of all time. The game was criticized for a lack of collision detection. Collision detection fixes the mistake that can happen when a character can get stuck in a wall, for example, or fall into an empty space.

Video games designers have to fix bugs in their design. They need to work hard to try and improve each game and keep up with any new methods and fixes.

## FACT FILE

Video game design students study the key concepts of game design, such as illustration, character design, and 3D modelling. They also learn game mechanics and how to think up concepts. Importantly they learn how to manage a project, too. In college, students will produce playable game prototypes. A prototype is a pre-production working model. Students then learn to test the prototypes to produce finished, playable video games.

A video game design degree is great training for the job. Students often get to meet industry professionals and present their work to them.

# Glossary

**animation** (a-nuh-MAY-shun)
A film made by photographing a series of positions of objects.

**arcades** (ar-KAYDZ)
Places with games to be played by putting coins in them.

**audio** (AH-dee-oh)
Of or relating to sound or its reproduction and especially accurate reproduction.

**concepts** (KON-septs)
General ideas.

**conferences** (KON-frun-sez)
Meetings for discussion or exchange of opinions.

**consoles** (KON-sohlz)
Control panels for electronic devices.

**deadline** (DED-lyn)
A date or time before which something must be done.

**disabilities**
(dis-uh-BIH-luh-teez)
The lack of ability, power, or fitness to do something.

**genres** (ZHON-ruhz)
Types or categories of game.

**graphics** (GRA-fiks)
Images generated by a computer.

**internships** (IN-turn-ships)
Practical on-the-job experience.

**narrative** (NER-uh-tiv)
The video game's storyline.

**network** (NET-wurk)
To make connections with people in the industry.

**pixels** (PIK-sulz)
The small elements that together make up an image.

**portfolio**
(port-FOH-lee-oh)
Examples of work done.

**programming**
(PROH-gram-ing)
The design and production of computer programs.

**storyboarding**
(STOR-ee-bord-ing)
Producing a sequence of drawings representing the story of the game.

**texture** (TEKS-chur)
The structure, feel, and appearance of something.

**tutorials** (too-TOR-ee-ulz)
Practical lessons about a subject.

**villains** (VIL-unz)
Characters in a story or play who oppose the hero.

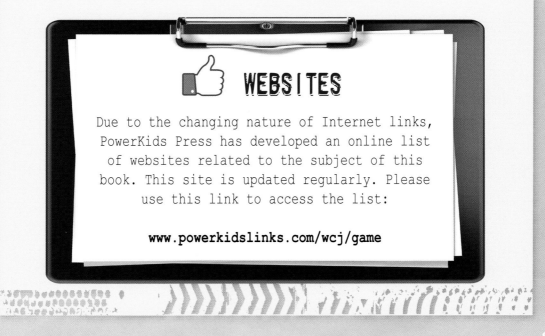

## WEBSITES

Due to the changing nature of Internet links, PowerKids Press has developed an online list of websites related to the subject of this book. This site is updated regularly. Please use this link to access the list:

**www.powerkidslinks.com/wcj/game**

# Read More

Funk, Joe. *Hot Jobs in Video Games.* Cool Careers in Interactive Entertainment. New York: Scholastic, 2010.

Maltman, Thomas James. *The Electrifying, Action-Packed, Unusual History of Video Games.* Mankato, MN: Capstone Press, 2011.

Sturm, Jeanne. *Video Games.* Let's Explore Science. Vero Beach, FL: Rourke Publishing, 2010.

# Index